Original title:
Love's Fulfillment

Copyright © 2024 Swan Charm
All rights reserved.

Author: Paula Raudsepp
ISBN HARDBACK: 978-9916-89-340-1
ISBN PAPERBACK: 978-9916-89-341-8
ISBN EBOOK: 978-9916-89-342-5

In the Shadow of Your Light

In the twilight softly gleaming,
Your presence wraps like a cloak.
Whispers of dreams now are streaming,
In silence, my heart's words evoke.

Moments dance with silver grace,
Beneath the stars, our secrets blend.
In the stillness, I find your trace,
Guiding me like a steadfast friend.

Together we chase the fading sun,
Hand in hand, through twilight's embrace.
With every heartbeat, we become one,
No shadows can dim this sacred space.

Your laughter sparkles like the dawn,
Chasing the night away with light.
In the depths, I feel reborn,
In the shadow of your sweet insight.

As the moon oversees our plight,
The world melts into hues of night.
In the shelter of your delight,
I find solace, pure and bright.

The Milestones of Our Odyssey

We set sail on seas unknown,
With stars as guides, dreams in our eyes.
Each wave a tale of seeds we've sown,
In realms where hope and courage rise.

A lighthouse glimmers on the shore,
A beacon for our wandering hearts.
With each milestone, we seek for more,
Drawing maps where adventure starts.

Through storms we've braved with grit and grace,
Our bond unyielding, strong as steel.
In every challenge, we find our place,
Together, we'll conquer, together we'll heal.

The horizon calls, a distant song,
A melody of ages past.
In unity, we can't go wrong,
For in each other, we find the vast.

With every step, a story grows,
In laughter's echoes, tears that flow.
Through the journeys that life bestows,
The milestones mark love's endless glow.

The Sweetness of Our Journey

We wander through fields where flowers bloom,
Laughter echoes in the softest room.
Hand in hand, we trace the sky,
Each step forward, a whispered sigh.

The sun sets low, a golden trace,
In your eyes, I find my place.
Memories weave in twilight's glow,
With every heartbeat, our love will grow.

As stars begin to light the night,
Our dreams take flight, a wondrous sight.
Through valleys deep and mountains wide,
Together we journey, side by side.

Harmonies of a Quiet Promise

In the stillness, a gentle song,
Where two souls learn to belong.
Words unspoken, yet so clear,
In this moment, you're always near.

The world around us fades away,
In your gaze, I long to stay.
Every heartbeat sings our truth,
A harmony that holds our youth.

With whispers soft, we forge ahead,
On paths of love where dreams are fed.
A quiet promise, strong and bright,
Guides us through the darkest night.

Candlelight Conversations

Flickering flames dance on the wall,
In your eyes, I see it all.
Words are woven, warm and slow,
In candlelight, our feelings glow.

Laughter spills like molten gold,
In this space, our dreams unfold.
Every story, every sigh,
With you, time just passes by.

The shadows play, the night is young,
In this moment, we are one.
With gentle touches, silence speaks,
In candlelight, our love seeks.

A Tapestry of Togetherness

Threads of life entwine with grace,
In every moment, I find your face.
Colors merge and softly blend,
In this tapestry, no end.

Each shared laugh, each tender tear,
Stitches memories we hold dear.
With every row, our hearts align,
Woven tightly, your hand in mine.

Through storms that swirl and skies that clear,
In togetherness, we conquer fear.
A masterpiece crafted with our care,
In this woven love, we'll always share.

Bridge of Intentions

Upon the arch we step so light,
With whispers soft, our dreams take flight.
Each heartbeat bridges wide and far,
Guiding us true, our shining star.

We meet in shadows cast by fate,
Where hopes and wishes intertwine straight.
The winds of change begin to call,
Together we rise, we shall not fall.

In every stride, intentions clear,
We build this path, hold what's dear.
Brick by brick, a bond we weave,
A promise made, we dare believe.

Look at the sky, our canvas bright,
Painting our future in beams of light.
For on this bridge, we find our way,
Through every night and every day.

Reflections of Trust

In quiet pools, our dreams reside,
Mirrors of truth where hearts confide.
With every glance, we share our fears,
A journey forged across the years.

The gentle waves of trust we share,
Lift us softly, aware, laid bare.
In love's embrace, we find our peace,
A sanctuary where doubts cease.

In every tear, a message flows,
Translucent, pure, as the stillness grows.
With every smile, we seal our fate,
Bound by a thread we won't abate.

The sun will rise, the shadows fall,
Yet through it all, we stand tall.
With laughter's echo and silence's grace,
In the reflection, we find our place.

Hearts Entwined

Two souls converge, their paths align,
In tangled roots where love will shine.
With every beat, a rhythm flows,
In perfect time, our being grows.

The warmth of hands, a gentle touch,
In this embrace, we have so much.
With silent vows, our spirits soar,
Together forever, we crave more.

Like vines that cling to strength and grace,
In each other's arms, we find our space.
A dance of hearts, a whispered song,
In the silence, we both belong.

Through stormy seas and skies so bright,
We'll navigate by love's true light.
In every pulse, a promise sewn,
In our entwined hearts, we are home.

The Pulse of Forever

In echoes deep, we hear the sound,
Of love's great pulse that knows no bound.
Each moment shared, a timeless beat,
A symphony where hearts repeat.

Through ages past and dreams foretold,
A story rich, in whispers bold.
The threads of fate will weave and spin,
In every loss, new joys begin.

With hands held tight, we face the dawn,
Together strong, we carry on.
In twilight's glow, forever's call,
We promise love will conquer all.

With every breath, the world's anew,
In every glance, it's me and you.
For as we pulse, a truth we find,
In endless love, our hearts aligned.

Lighthouse of Heartbeats

In the darkness, we find light,
A beacon shining through the night.
Each heartbeat tells a tale anew,
Guiding my soul, always to you.

Waves crash, yet we stand firm,
In the storm, our passions churn.
A lighthouse whispering to the sea,
Your heart, my safe sanctuary.

With every pulse, a rhythm flows,
In this dance, our love just grows.
Tides may change, but we stay true,
Anchored deep, just me and you.

Silent vows in the moon's glow,
In the current, love begins to grow.
Through every tempest, every scar,
You are my light, my shining star.

So let the winds and waters rage,
Together we'll turn every page.
For in the lighthouse, hearts align,
Bound forever, your heart in mine.

As Seasons Change

Leaves fall softly to the ground,
In crisp air, new joys are found.
Autumn whispers, golden and bright,
A tapestry of day and night.

Winter blankets all we see,
Cold and still, yet warm are we.
By the fire, stories we share,
In the chill, our hearts lay bare.

Spring arrives with colors bold,
New beginnings, dreams untold.
Flowers bloom beneath the sun,
In this season, we're just begun.

Summer calls, heat in the air,
Laughter echoes everywhere.
Days grow long, and moments sweet,
In the sun, our hearts compete.

Each season turns, a flowing dance,
Love renews with every chance.
As time unfolds, our bond will grow,
Through every season, this we know.

Hidden Depths of Us

Beneath the surface, secrets lie,
In quiet waters, dreams do sigh.
The depths of us, a tranquil sea,
Endless whispers, just you and me.

In shadows cast by doubt and fear,
We find the light that draws us near.
Exploring realms, both vast and deep,
Together, our heart's secrets keep.

With every breath, the currents change,
Uncharted waters feel so strange.
Yet in the unknown, we can trust,
Our love will guide through every gust.

Through storms that rise and winds that blow,
In hidden depths, our passions flow.
A journey taken, hand in hand,
In silent depths, we make our stand.

So let the world fade into night,
In hidden depths, we find our light.
For in the dark, our souls ignite,
In each other's arms, all feels right.

The Map of Our Journey

A journey drawn on weathered maps,
With every turn, our love perhaps.
Paths entwined beneath the skies,
In every step, a new surprise.

Mountains steep, and valleys wide,
Side by side, we take the ride.
With every mile, our spirits soar,
In this adventure, we explore.

Through forests thick and rivers clear,
With every heartbeat, I draw near.
The compass spins, but still we roam,
In your heart, I've found my home.

With every star that lights the night,
We'll chart our course, our future bright.
No destination too far or grand,
Together, we'll dream, hand in hand.

So let the currents lead us forth,
In every season, every worth.
For on this map, we boldly tread,
In love's embrace, our souls are fed.

Charting the Course of Affection

In the map of you and me,
We find our hearts align.
Through storms and sunlit seas,
Our love's a steady line.

With every whispered word,
We navigate the night.
Your gaze, a guiding star,
In darkness, you're my light.

We'll sail through troubled tides,
With faith as our refrain.
Together, side by side,
We'll weather every gain.

The compass of our trust,
Points toward the unknown.
As passion leads the way,
In this sea, we have grown.

With each shared moment's bliss,
We chart a brand new course.
In love's vast wilderness,
Together we're the force.

The Echo of Your Laugh

Your laughter lights the room,
It dances in the air.
Like ripples on a lake,
It banishes my care.

In moments soft and sweet,
The echoes intertwine.
They weave a melody,
That feels so purely divine.

In corridors of time,
Your joy forever plays.
A symphony of light,
That brightens all my days.

Each giggle, like a spark,
Ignites the darkest night.
In the sound of your glee,
I find immense delight.

With every laugh we share,
My heart begins to soar.
In the echo of your joy,
I wish for nothing more.

The Roots of Our Togetherness

In a garden deeply sown,
Our roots begin to blend.
Each laughter, tear, and joy,
A tie that will not end.

With every shared belief,
We grow in strength and grace.
Together as we bloom,
In love's tight embrace.

The seasons may change us,
But our bond remains true.
Through shadows and through light,
I will stand here for you.

As branches intertwine,
Our stories intertwine too.
In the soil of our love,
We nurture all that's new.

With roots that run so deep,
Forever intertwined.
In this garden of trust,
Our souls are well defined.

Embracing the Infinite Now

In the stillness of this breath,
We find a world anew.
The chaos fades away,
As we embrace what's true.

Each fleeting moment's grace,
Is captured in our hearts.
In the dance of now,
A timeless work of art.

Through whispers and through sighs,
We trace the lines of fate.
In the infinite now,
Our souls resonant, elate.

With eyes wide open wide,
We savor every glance.
In the magic of this time,
We lose ourselves in chance.

Here's to love's embrace,
In this moment, we rise.
As the now unfolds,
We bask in love's disguise.

A Heartfelt Compass

In every whisper, love's gentle call,
Guiding me through shadows, never to fall.
Your laughter lights the darkest of skies,
A compass of hope, where our dream lies.

Together we wander, hand in hand,
Mapping the pathways of this sacred land.
With every heartbeat, our story unfolds,
A treasure of moments, more precious than gold.

In storms we find shelter, in peace, we dance,
Crafting a melody born from our chance.
The stars above witness our journey, so bright,
A guiding compass, our love's constant light.

Through every season, the branches may sway,
But roots intertwine, they hold us at bay.
In the forest of time, our hearts intertwine,
A tale everlasting, eternally thine.

Into the Depths of Togetherness

In the quiet moments, we breathe as one,
Shared dreams whisper softly, like rays of the sun.
Through laughter and tears, our bond only grows,
Strengthening roots in the soil that we chose.

Two hearts entwined, in rhythm they beat,
Dancing through life, where challenges meet.
With trust as our anchor, we sail through the storm,
In the embrace of togetherness, we find our warm.

Each glance is a treasure, each word a delight,
Crafting our path, as we venture in light.
In the depths of connection, we make our stand,
Together forever, hand in hand.

Through valleys of silence and mountains of sound,
In unity's heart, our spirits are bound.
Into the depths, where few dare to tread,
We cultivate love, where angels have led.

Unseen Textures of Devotion

In whispers of night, where shadows softly weave,
The texture of love speaks, though seldom perceived.
Each glance, a soft thread, each smile, a warm hue,
Woven together, our tapestry grew.

Fingers entwined, through seasons, we glide,
In the fabric of trust, we steadily bide.
Weathers may change, but our colors hold true,
Unseen devotion, a bond tried and true.

In quiet encounters, our spirits converse,
Exploring the depths, as we learn to immerse.
With patience, we carve our names in the stars,
Unseen textures of love, delicate scars.

Through the years we weave, in patterns unique,
The language of hearts, it's connection we seek.
In moments of stillness, we silently vow,
An art of devotion, living in the now.

The Rhythm of Our Steps

Each step we take, the world dances anew,
In harmony's pulse, me and you.
With laughter and love as our guiding beat,
We walk through this life, in sync and complete.

Amidst the soft whispers of night's gentle breeze,
We find our own rhythm, moving with ease.
In the silence of moments, our hearts choreograph,
A timeless duet, in joy and in laugh.

From dawn until dusk, our journey unfolds,
In the steps we embrace, our story is told.
With every misstep, we learn and we grow,
Creating a melody, a sweet ebb and flow.

Together, we waltz through the trials we face,
With courage and grace, we set our own pace.
In the rhythm of our steps, we find our way,
A dance of forever, come what may.

The Infinite We

In the starry sky we meet,
Two souls in harmony,
Bound by dreams so sweet,
Together, wild and free.

Through rivers deep we glide,
Hand in hand, side by side,
In whispers soft we confide,
With the world, we collide.

Moments woven like a thread,
In laughter, joy, and cheer,
Each word lovingly said,
Our path forever clear.

With every dawn we rise,
Chasing shadows of the past,
In your gaze, love lies,
A bond that's built to last.

Through storms and sunlit days,
Our hearts beat the same song,
In this dance, love sways,
Together we belong.

Moonlight Reflections

Beneath the silvery glow,
Whispers float on the breeze,
In the night, dreams flow,
Carried through the trees.

The soft moonlight does play,
On waters calm and clear,
Lighting our gentle way,
With love lingering near.

Stars twinkle in delight,
As we share our tales,
In the quiet night,
Hope in every exhale.

Each moment we embrace,
In the shadows, we dance,
Finding our sacred space,
In this timeless romance.

With the dawn we awake,
Memories etched in gold,
In every choice we make,
Our story will be told.

Heartbeats in Unison

Two hearts in perfect sync,
With every pulse, we thrive,
In moments on the brink,
Together we arrive.

Through laughter and through tears,
Our rhythm guides the way,
Facing all our fears,
In love, we choose to stay.

In the dance of the night,
Every step feels so right,
We shine like stars so bright,
In each other's light.

Bound by threads unseen,
A tapestry of dreams,
In spaces in-between,
Love flows in gentle streams.

Our voices softly blend,
In echoes of the past,
With you, I will transcend,
Together, love stands fast.

An Ode to Us

In the quiet of the dawn,
Two souls intertwine,
With a love that's been drawn,
A masterpiece divine.

Through trials we have grown,
With every tear and smile,
In this garden we've sown,
Love blossoms all the while.

From whispers to a shout,
Our story finds its way,
In the heart where doubt,
Gives way to light of day.

With every breath we take,
In the tapestry of time,
A bond that cannot break,
Together, we will climb.

So here's to dreams we chase,
In this journey we share,
In every warm embrace,
An ode to love laid bare.

The Mosaic of Shared Lives

In colors bright, we weave our fate,
Each thread a moment, love won't wait.
Unique and rare, our stories blend,
A tapestry where hearts transcend.

Together we laugh, together we cry,
With whispered dreams and hopes so high.
In shades of joy, in hues of pain,
We find each other again, again.

Through trials faced and paths we roam,
In every heart, we find a home.
Each experience, a stroke of grace,
In life's grand art, our sacred space.

As seasons change, our colors may fade,
But in every heart, our love is laid.
We're stronger now, as we evolve,
In this mosaic, our lives resolve.

A Journey in Bloom

With each new dawn, the petals rise,
A fragrant burst beneath the skies.
Bright colors dance, a sight to see,
In nature's arms, we're wild and free.

Through winding paths, our hopes take flight,
In fields of green, we chase the light.
Each step we take, a blossom blooms,
With every heartbeat, new life looms.

In vibrant hues, our spirits soar,
Embracing change, we yearn for more.
Together we stand, both strong and true,
Through storms and sun, our love renews.

As challenges rise, and fears may loom,
We'll face it together, our hearts in tune.
In this garden, our dreams entwined,
Our journey in bloom, forever kind.

Unwritten Chapters of Our Tale

With every heartbeat, a page unfolds,
In silent whispers, our story's told.
Unwritten chapters wait to be penned,
In this grand book, we'll never end.

Moments shared, like stars that gleam,
In the quiet night, we dare to dream.
Through laughter's echoes and tears we trace,
In every line, we find our place.

We write in ink of hopes and fears,
Of joy that sparkles and hidden tears.
The plot will twist, but love remains,
In every story, our heart retains.

A tapestry woven with threads of time,
In verses whispered, our souls will climb.
Beyond the words, a bond so real,
Unwritten chapters, it's ours to seal.

The Pulse of Connection

In every heartbeat, a bond is found,
A silent rhythm, our souls unbound.
Through whispered dreams and laughter shared,
In tender moments, our hearts laid bare.

To feel your presence is to ignite,
A flame that flickers in the night.
With every glance, a spark will glow,
In our embrace, the world will slow.

Distance may stretch, but love will glue,
Across the miles, I'm close to you.
In every heartbeat, we resonate,
In this pulse of life, we celebrate.

As life unfolds, and challenges sway,
We stand together, come what may.
With gentle strength, our spirits align,
In the pulse of connection, forever shine.

Light in Your Eyes

In the stillness of the night,
I see the stars align,
Their shimmer soft and bright,
Reflecting love divine.

Your gaze, a guiding spark,
Illuminates my way,
It banishes the dark,
Turns night to radiant day.

With every smile you share,
The world feels full of grace,
I find you everywhere,
In every warm embrace.

Your laughter, a sweet song,
That dances in my mind,
Together we belong,
Two souls forever intertwined.

In the light within your eyes,
Hope and joy unite,
A love that never dies,
Our hearts forever bright.

Bound by Dreams

In whispered thoughts, we soar,
Through realms both wide and free,
Chasing dreams we can't ignore,
Together, you and me.

With every star we chase,
We weave our destined tale,
In this timeless space,
Where hearts, they never fail.

Hand in hand we explore,
The wonders yet to find,
In this dream's allure,
Our spirits intertwined.

The night holds secret truths,
That guide us on our way,
Embracing all the youth,
In moments we relay.

With every dream we share,
The boundaries fall away,
We'll brave the storms we dare,
Love leads us, come what may.

The Harmony of Hearts

In a world of gentle sounds,
Two hearts begin to play,
In rhythms that astound,
Creating night and day.

Each beat a soft refrain,
Echoes in the air,
A melody so plain,
Carried everywhere.

Together we compose,
A symphony so sweet,
In every hush and prose,
Our souls begin to meet.

With grace, we dance along,
The paths we both have chose,
In harmony, so strong,
Together, love bestows.

As notes entwine and weave,
Our hearts forever blend,
In silence, we believe,
A love that has no end.

Threads of Affection

In the tapestry of life,
We weave our dreams around,
Each thread, a joy or strife,
In colors, love is found.

With gentle hands, we stitch,
Creating every scene,
Through every little niche,
Our hearts form a routine.

Although the world may tear,
These threads will hold us close,
Through trials we will bear,
In love, we find our boast.

With each soft touch and sigh,
Our bonds become so strong,
Together, you and I,
In this dance, we belong.

As long as we shall be,
These threads shall never fray,
In the fabric of the sea,
Of love that lights the way.

Embrace of Forever

In twilight's glow, hearts entwine,
Promises whispered, soft and fine.
Time stands still, a gentle breath,
In this moment, love transcends death.

Stars above start to weave,
Dreams and hopes that we believe.
Hand in hand, we walk this path,
Together forging our own math.

Each heartbeat sings, a lullaby,
Underneath the endless sky.
Shadows dance, casting light,
In your arms, everything feels right.

The world fades, and it's just us,
In this embrace, there's no fuss.
Forever beckons, a sweet call,
With you, I know I have it all.

A journey shared, deep and wide,
In love's embrace, we will abide.
With each sunrise, new stories start,
Bound forever, we're never apart.

The Language of Connection

Words unspoken fill the air,
A glance exchanged, a silent care.
In every smile, the truth resides,
A bond so strong, it never hides.

Through laughter bright, we find our way,
In gentle touch, come what may.
Shared moments turn to timeless art,
Painting whispers upon the heart.

Fingers brushing, sparks ignite,
In the shadows, we find our light.
With every heartbeat, a tale unfolds,
An unbroken thread, a love life holds.

Understanding blooms, pure and clear,
In your eyes, I feel you near.
The song of souls, a sweet refrain,
Binding us through joy and pain.

Let's dance together, side by side,
In this connection, we shall ride.
With every moment, we create,
A love so deep, a destined fate.

Serenade of Souls

In starlit night, our spirits sing,
A melody that life can bring.
Notes of kindness, chords of grace,
In harmony, we find our place.

Each heartbeat strums a gentle tune,
Dancing lightly, like a moon.
Whispers float upon the breeze,
Serenade beneath the trees.

Together weaving dreams so bright,
Coloring shadows with our light.
Every glance, a verse we write,
In the quiet, love takes flight.

Through every trial, every woe,
Our song, a balm, begins to flow.
In laughter shared, the world ignites,
In our embrace, day turns to night.

Let's waltz upon the winds of fate,
In the serenade, we celebrate.
Bound by love, a sacred role,
In this dance, we find our soul.

Dance of Devotion

With rhythm strong, our hearts do sway,
In this dance, we find our way.
Steps aligned, like stars we twirl,
In every move, our love unfurls.

Underneath the watchful moon,
In silence, we hear our tune.
Each twirl and spin, a promise made,
In devotion, fears will fade.

Through dips and turns, we claim the night,
With every breath, a shared delight.
In the spotlight of our dreams,
Together, nothing's as it seems.

Whispers echo, joy ignites,
Our spirits soar to dizzy heights.
In the cadence of this chance,
Let's lose ourselves within this dance.

Fueled by passion, bold and true,
In this embrace, it's me and you.
Each moment cherished, we devote,
In our dance, love will float.

Serendipity Under Starlit Skies

Beneath a canvas painted bright,
We found each other, pure delight.
Whispers carried on the breeze,
Promises tangled in the trees.

Laughter mingled with the night,
Each moment felt just right.
Stars above, a guiding light,
Serendipitous our flight.

Hand in hand, we dream and play,
In this magical ballet.
With every twinkle, hearts ignite,
In the arms of purest night.

Time stands still, just you and me,
Floating on this reverie.
Every heartbeat sings a tune,
Dancing 'neath the watchful moon.

Our journey written in the skies,
A tapestry that never lies.
In this moment, love professed,
Together, we are truly blessed.

The Dance of Timeless Affection

In a world that spins so fast,
We hold each other, making moments last.
With every step, we weave our song,
In this dance, we both belong.

Eyes locked in a soulful glance,
Hearts entwined in a perfect dance.
Every twirl, a whispered vow,
We bask in love, here and now.

Sweet familiarity in each turn,
With you, my heart will always yearn.
Through shadows cast and light that plays,
Together we dance through endless days.

With every rhythm, love remains,
Filling our lives like gentle rains.
A melody that knows no end,
In each beat, my heart will send.

Hand in hand, we face the night,
With every step, our souls ignite.
In the dance of timeless affection,
Forever strong, our connection.

When Eyes Meet This Way

In a crowded room, time stands still,
When your eyes meet mine, I feel the thrill.
A spark ignites in the simple glance,
We share a moment, a silent romance.

Words unspoken yet so clear,
In your gaze, I lose all fear.
A universe within your sight,
When eyes meet this way, the world feels right.

A gentle pull, a magnetic force,
Drawing us near, like a river's course.
In the depths of your soulful hue,
I find the echoes of something true.

The universe aligns just so,
As our hearts dance to a rhythm slow.
In every blink, a tale unfolds,
A bond so deep, a heart of gold.

When the world fades away with time,
Your eyes, my muse, they hold the rhyme.
In this sacred, transient space,
We find forever in a fleeting gaze.

Kaleidoscope of Us

In every shade, a story shines,
A tapestry woven with love's designs.
Colors blending, hearts entwined,
In this kaleidoscope, our souls aligned.

Each twist reveals a new delight,
Fragments of joy in the soft moonlight.
Reflections dance, a vibrant hue,
A symphony played by me and you.

Moments captured, forever true,
In every glance, I see anew.
A beautiful chaos, wild and free,
In this kaleidoscope, just you and me.

Through storms and sunshine, we remain,
Painting our love through joy and pain.
A masterpiece crafted, hand in hand,
In our colorful world, we'll always stand.

With every shift, our love expands,
A dance of life, a blend of strands.
In every piece, a part of us,
A kaleidoscope of love, in trust.

The Art of Belonging

In shadows cast by ancient trees,
We find our roots, a gentle breeze.
With whispers soft and ties that bind,
A tapestry of hearts aligned.

Through laughter shared and silent tones,
We weave a tale of many homes.
In every glance and every sigh,
Together, we will learn to fly.

Embracing flaws, a sweet refrain,
In moments lost, in joy, in pain.
The art of love, a canvas bright,
With colors deep, we paint the night.

As seasons shift and rivers flow,
In every heart, a fire will grow.
The art of belonging, pure and true,
A bond unbreakable, me and you.

Unwritten Promises

Beneath the stars, where dreams ignite,
We carve our hopes in the still night.
With every glance, a vow we share,
Unwritten promises linger in the air.

In whispered tunes, our secrets blend,
A symphony with no clear end.
With tender words, we softly tread,
In silent pacts that never shred.

Through storms we face, hand in hand,
A silent trust, a steadfast strand.
The future's path may twist and sway,
But heartbeats echo what words can't say.

With every step, together we roam,
In hearts entwined, we build a home.
Unwritten promises, brave and bold,
Together we'll write our story told.

In Your Warmth

In quiet moments, I find my peace,
Your laugh, a melody, sweet release.
With every touch, the world grows bright,
In your warmth, my heart takes flight.

Through gentle nights and sunlit days,
Our love ignites in splendid ways.
Each glance exchanged, a spark ignites,
In your warmth, my soul delights.

When shadows loom and doubts arise,
In your embrace, I see the skies.
No storms can break what we create,
In your warmth, I find my fate.

With every heartbeat, every sigh,
Together, we learn how to fly.
In your warmth, I've found my song,
In love's embrace, we've always belonged.

Tides of Togetherness

Like waves that dance upon the shore,
Our hearts collide, forevermore.
With every rise, with every fall,
In tides of togetherness, we stand tall.

Through whispered secrets, soft and true,
We navigate the ocean blue.
In laughter's echo, we find our way,
With every tide, we softly sway.

In harmony, we face the storm,
In unity, we find our form.
With every heartbeat, every bind,
In tides of love, our souls aligned.

Through rolling waves and gentle streams,
We chase our hopes, fulfill our dreams.
Together bound like sea and sand,
In tides of togetherness, we stand.

Beyond the Stars

In the vast expanse we see,
Endless wonders call to me.
Whispers of the night unfold,
Stories of the brave and bold.

Celestial bodies dance and shine,
Drawing us in, a cosmic line.
Dreams ignite like shooting stars,
Guiding our way, no matter how far.

Through the black, a light so bright,
Sparkles in the endless night.
We reach for hope, for peace, for fate,
Beyond the stars, we contemplate.

Veils of mystery intertwine,
In the silence, we define.
A universe of hearts and minds,
In harmony, our purpose finds.

So let us drift where dreams reside,
With every wish, a cosmic guide.
In the vast expanse, we roam,
Together, we will call it home.

In the Light of Us

In shadows cast, we find our way,
Illuminated by love's soft sway.
A gentle glow, a vibrant spark,
Together we shine, even in dark.

Through every storm, we face as one,
Our dreams ignite, a rising sun.
In whispered secrets, souls align,
In the light of us, our hearts combine.

Moments shared, like golden rays,
Creating warmth in the coldest days.
Through laughter and through gentle sighs,
In each other's gaze, our future lies.

Time may bend, but love stays true,
In every breath, it's me and you.
Together we dance, as time flows past,
In this light of us, forever cast.

So hand in hand, let us embrace,
No darkness found in our sacred space.
For in this life, amidst the fuss,
We find our peace, in the light of us.

The Garden of Emotions

In the garden where feelings bloom,
Petals whisper, dispel all gloom.
Each flower tells a story sweet,
A tapestry where hearts can meet.

Joy like daisies, bright and bold,
Memories of laughter, stories told.
Sadness lingers, weeping willow,
In its shade, we find our pillow.

Love's deep rose, with thorns to guard,
Tenderness weaves, a path not hard.
Anger like storms, fierce and strong,
Yet after the rain, we learn to belong.

Hope like seedlings, reaching high,
In the sunlight, they touch the sky.
Fears like shadows, fade with grace,
In this garden, we find our place.

So tend this space, with care and grace,
Let emotions flourish in their trace.
For in this garden, we shall see,
The beauty that sets our spirits free.

A Symphony of Two

In harmony we find our song,
A rhythm where we both belong.
With every note, a tale we weave,
In this melody, we believe.

Two voices rise, a perfect blend,
An echo of love that will not end.
In laughter and tears, the music flows,
A symphony that only we know.

Through crescendos and gentle sighs,
In the space where magic lies.
With chords that resonate so true,
In this world, it's me and you.

Each heartbeat a drum, steady and loud,
In the silence, we're drawing a crowd.
With every dance, each gentle sway,
A masterpiece in our own way.

So let us play, let us explore,
A symphony of dreams, forevermore.
For in this life, as we compose,
Together, our love beautifully grows.

The Art of Building Dreams Together

In twilight's glow, we sketch our fate,
With whispered hopes, we celebrate.
Each careful line, together drawn,
We build our world from dusk till dawn.

Brick by brick, our visions rise,
A tapestry beneath the skies.
Hands in hands, we shape the clay,
Creating love in our own way.

With colors bright, we paint our days,
In laughter's sound, in gentle praise.
Two souls unite, with heart and mind,
In this great dance, our dreams entwined.

As seasons change, our plans expand,
In every step, we understand.
Together we'll face the winds and rain,
For through it all, love will remain.

With every brick, a story told,
In silent nights, in moments bold.
The art of dreams is ours to share,
In harmony, beyond compare.

Two Hearts, One Melody

Together we sway, in rhythm divine,
Two hearts beat as one, a perfect sign.
In every glance, a song is sung,
A melody sweet, forever young.

With gentle notes, our voices blend,
In laughter's echo, love transcends.
Through highs and lows, our chorus plays,
A dance of souls, through endless days.

In quiet moments, our bond grows tight,
With whispered dreams in the soft moonlight.
Like stars above, we shine so bright,
Two hearts united, a glorious sight.

The rhythm guides us, side by side,
In this journey, our hearts confide.
With every step, our lives compose,
A symphony where true love flows.

So hand in hand, together we'll go,
Through life's great stage, the ebb and flow.
In every beat, our spirits soar,
Two hearts, one melody, forevermore.

In the Prism of Affection

Love refracts through a crystal lens,
In every hue, our story blends.
From tender touch to softest sigh,
In the prism of affection, we fly.

Each color shines in radiant light,
Casting shadows, embracing night.
Hearts intertwined, a dance of grace,
In this kaleidoscope, we find our place.

The moments shared, like rainbows bright,
In laughter's glow and passion's flight.
A spectrum vast, our spirits trace,
In the prism of affection's embrace.

Through trials faced, we stand as one,
In hues of hope, our fears undone.
With every layer, deeper we see,
In love's reflection, we're truly free.

So let the colors swirl and play,
In the light of love, we'll find our way.
In every shade, our hearts will sing,
In the prism of affection, forever spring.

Astral Paths Intertwined

In the heavens high, our fates align,
With stardust whispers, we intertwine.
Galaxies spin, in cosmic ballet,
Astral paths lead us, come what may.

Through nebulae bright, our hopes ignite,
As constellations guide through the night.
In the quiet cosmos, our dreams expand,
Together we soar, hand in hand.

Each star a promise, a memory bright,
Illuminating love, our guiding light.
Across the universe, we chart our course,
Two souls united, a powerful force.

In gravitational pull, our hearts connect,
Venturing forth with deep respect.
Through solar winds that softly blow,
In boundless skies, our spirits flow.

With every orbit, our bond will grow,
In the fabric of space, we find our glow.
In astral realms, as timeless we find,
Our destinies woven, forever entwined.

Threads of Destiny

In the tapestry of time, we weave,
Moments glimmer like stars that believe.
Each thread pulled tight, a story to tell,
In the fabric of fate, we dwell.

Winds of change blow soft and low,
Guiding our paths where love can grow.
Every twist and turn, a choice we make,
In this dance of life, our hearts awake.

Golden threads shine in the light,
Binding us close, making it right.
Through joy and sorrow, we understand,
Together we stand, hand in hand.

Fate's needle stitches with gentle grace,
Time's embrace in a warm space.
Eager hearts, forever aligned,
Threads of destiny, beautifully entwined.

As the pattern unfolds, we find our way,
In the loom of existence, we will stay.
Forever woven, our spirits free,
Threads of destiny, you and me.

The Odyssey of Together

Through the waves of time, we sail,
With whispered dreams, we will prevail.
The journey long, but hearts are bright,
In the odyssey, we find our light.

Hand in hand, we face the storm,
In each embrace, our spirits warm.
Navigating shores of hopes and fears,
Together we conquer, through all the years.

Stars above guide our way anew,
In the night sky, our love shines through.
On this voyage, both fierce and sweet,
Every moment shared, a treasured beat.

With every challenge, a bond we gain,
In the laughter and in the pain.
The compass points to where we belong,
In harmony, we grow ever strong.

As the waves kiss the golden sand,
Together we'll rise, forever we stand.
In the odyssey, our hearts ignite,
Boundless love, our guiding light.

Whispers of Heart's Embrace

A gentle breeze through the trees,
Brings tender whispers, soft as these.
In silken tones, our secrets flow,
Whispers of heart's embrace we know.

In quiet moments, two souls unite,
Across the distance, infinite light.
Your laughter dances on my skin,
In heart's caress, our journey begins.

Eyes that sparkle like morning dew,
In their gaze, a world so true.
With every heartbeat, I hear the call,
Whispers shared, we have it all.

Silent vows beneath the stars,
In this embrace, we heal our scars.
Together we rise, forever bold,
In the warmth of love, our story unfolds.

As the moon cradles the night so dear,
With every whisper, I hold you near.
In the silence, our souls entwine,
Whispers of heart's embrace, divine.

A Symphony of Two Souls

In the hush of dusk, a melody plays,
Two souls dance in a sweet haze.
Every note a story, soft and bright,
In the symphony, our hearts take flight.

With every heartbeat, a rhythm is found,
Together we sing, our spirits unbound.
In harmony, we echo the tune,
A love that blossoms beneath the moon.

Strings intertwined, so rich and pure,
In this overture, we feel secure.
With every glance, a heartbeat sings,
In our duet, the world still swings.

As crescendos rise, we soar so high,
Two souls entwined, we touch the sky.
In this masterpiece, forever we play,
A symphony of love, come what may.

Through the silence, our laughter rings,
With every heartbeat, the joy it brings.
In the concert of life, let love enroll,
Together forever, a symphony of soul.

The Craft of Our Dreams

In quiet rooms, we weave our thoughts,
With threads of hope, as time is caught.
Each stitch a wish, a vibrant hue,
Creating worlds where dreams come true.

In whispered tales, we shape the night,
With stars above, our guiding light.
We mold the clay of untold fate,
Crafting a future, intricate, great.

Hands intertwined, we paint the sky,
With colors bold, we learn to fly.
Each canvas shared, we learn to see,
The endless possibilities, you and me.

In every doubt, we find our voice,
Together forging, a shared choice.
Through trials faced, our spirits climb,
Building our dreams, one step at a time.

Tides of Connection

The ocean's pulse calls out to me,
A melody of harmony.
Waves embrace, a soft caress,
In this dance, we find our rest.

Beneath the stars, we drift and sway,
In the night's embrace, we learn to play.
The moon's reflection glints so bright,
Guiding us through the velvet night.

With every wave, a story unfolds,
Of shores we've walked, and hearts turned bold.
The current pulls, yet we hold fast,
In tides of connection, our love's steadfast.

The whispers of the wind, so sweet,
Carry our dreams on rhythmic beat.
Together we sail, through calm and storm,
In the ocean's arms, we find our form.

The Fireflies of Shared Secrets

In twilight's glow, they start to dance,
Fireflies twinkle, a fleeting chance.
Secrets shared in the fading light,
Illuminating the deepening night.

With laughter soft, we trace the air,
In every flicker, a whispered care.
Moments captured, like stars in a jar,
We hold them close, no matter how far.

Each glimmer brightens the shadows cast,
In this secret world, time moves fast.
In tender glances, our hearts align,
Amongst the fireflies, your hand in mine.

As dreams awaken with dawn's soft sigh,
We cherish the night, as time slips by.
In the light of day, our trust still glows,
Like fireflies dancing, love only grows.

A Summit of Two Hearts

High above, where eagles soar,
We climb together, seeking more.
The summit calls, a distant sight,
With every step, we share our light.

The rocks may crumble, the path may wane,
But side by side, we face the rain.
Our laughter echoes through the trees,
In nature's arms, we find our ease.

With every breath, the world stretches wide,
On this journey, we take in stride.
The view expands, our spirits rise,
Two hearts united beneath the skies.

As the sun sets and stars unveil,
We find our strength, in love we prevail.
A summit reached, together we stand,
Hand in hand, on this sacred land.

As Gentle as the Dawn

The sun peeks shyly, golden light,
Whispers of warmth, soft and bright.
Cool dew clings to blades of grass,
A silent promise—moments pass.

Birds begin their morning song,
In nature's arms, we all belong.
A canvas painted in pastel hues,
Awakening dreams, fresh and new.

Gentle breezes brush my face,
In this tranquil, sacred space.
Time is still; the world is wide,
As gentle as the dawn, our guide.

Each new day a chance to start,
With open hands and a hopeful heart.
Take a breath, let worries cease,
In dawn's embrace, we find our peace.

A Promise in Every Breath

Inhale the dreams that call your name,
Exhale the fears, let go of shame.
Each breath holds a chance to believe,
In the magic of moments, we weave.

A promise lies deep within,
In every day, where we begin.
Whispers of hope in the quietest air,
Together we rise, beyond compare.

Every heartbeat sings a tune,
Beneath the stars, beneath the moon.
Find strength in love, in laughter's grace,
A promise that time can't erase.

With courage and trust, we stand tall,
Together, we conquer, together, we fall.
In each shared moment, find your truth,
A promise in every breath, our youth.

Your Smile, My Anchor

In the storm, your smile shines bright,
A beacon of warmth in the darkest night.
Every glance fills me with peace,
In your presence, all worries cease.

Like a lighthouse guiding me home,
Through turbulent seas, no need to roam.
Your laughter, a melody sweet and clear,
A harmony born from love sincere.

When shadows linger and doubts arise,
Your smile's the sun that lights the skies.
Steady and strong, my refuge, my friend,
In the dance of life, together we bend.

With you beside me, I can dare,
To journey forth, to dream and share.
Your smile, my anchor, forever true,
In every heartbeat, I find you.

Beyond the Edge of Tomorrow

Whispers of time float on the breeze,
A tapestry woven with hopes that tease.
Each moment a doorway, a chance to explore,
Beyond the edge of tomorrow, there's more.

With courage to leap, we chase the sky,
Through valleys of doubt, we learn to fly.
Infinite paths lie beneath our feet,
In the rhythm of life, we find our beat.

Let dreams unfurl in vibrant light,
Paint the shadows with colors bright.
Embrace the unknown, let spirits roam,
Beyond the edge of tomorrow, we find home.

In the dance of time, we take our chance,
In every heartbeat, in every glance.
Together we journey, hand in hand,
Beyond the edge of tomorrow, we stand.

The Quiet Strength of Us

In silence, we find our place,
Together, we face time's grace.
Two hearts beat, a steady drum,
A bond unbroken, we become.

Through storms that shake and winds that wail,
Our roots run deep, we will not fail.
In every challenge, hand in hand,
We know together we will stand.

Soft words exchanged, a gentle touch,
In small moments, we find so much.
With every laugh and every tear,
Our quiet strength draws us near.

Though shadows may sometimes creep in,
With faith, we rise, together win.
For in this dance, we find our way,
In quiet strength, we choose to stay.

So let the world roar, loud and bright,
We hold our ground, we are the light.
Through whispered hopes and dreams we've sown,
In the quiet strength of us, we've grown.

In the Heart of the Moment

Time suspends, we breathe as one,
Each heartbeat echoes, just begun.
In stolen glances, worlds align,
Together here, your hand in mine.

The ticking clock fades to a hum,
In this embrace, a song's soft strum.
We share a laugh, a fleeting sigh,
In the heart of now, we learn to fly.

Each second blossoms, rich and rare,
In laughter's warmth, we shed our care.
Moments glow like stars at night,
In the heart of the moment, we find light.

A whisper shared, the world's afar,
In your eyes, I see a star.
Together we write, a tale so sweet,
In this rhythm, our hearts beat.

Let worries fade, let futures wait,
In this heartbeat, it's never late.
For in the now, a treasure stays,
In the heart of the moment, love displays.

Embracing the Beautiful Ordinary

In morning light, the world awakes,
With coffee smiles and gentle breaks.
Each simple moment, rich and clear,
In ordinary, we hold dear.

Worn paths we tread, familiar ground,
In every glance, new joy is found.
Every laugh, every shared meal,
In beautiful ordinary, we reveal.

The rustling leaves, a gentle breeze,
In nature's grace, our hearts find ease.
Through daily tasks, love's thread we weave,
In every hug, we dare believe.

Long walks beneath the stretch of skies,
In ordinary, magic lies.
Together in this life we share,
Each moment cherished, each heart laid bare.

So here's to life's mundane delight,
In simple joys, our spirits light.
For in embracing days, we see,
The beautiful ordinary, you and me.

Whispers in the Breeze

The wind carries secrets untold,
In rustling leaves, stories unfold.
With every breath, nature speaks clear,
In whispers of love, we draw near.

Mountains stand proud, skies stretch wide,
In nature's arms, we find our guide.
Each gust that dances through the trees,
Holds echoes of laughter, soft as these.

Fleeting moments drift by like clouds,
In every heart, joy's laughter loud.
Listen closely, hear the song,
In whispers, we know where we belong.

As dusk begins to paint the sky,
Stars emerge, where dreams soar high.
In twilight's hush and gentle peace,
The whispers in the breeze never cease.

So close your eyes and feel it flow,
In every sigh, our love does grow.
For in the world's sweet serenade,
In whispers in the breeze, we've made.

Echoes of Forever

Whispers of time drift softly near,
Memories wrapped in shadows dear.
Each heartbeat sings a gentle tune,
Echoes linger beneath the moon.

Waves of laughter, moments shared,
In the silence, love declared.
Through the storms, we'll always stay,
Echoes of forever guide our way.

Fleeting glances, a lingering smile,
Time transforms each weary mile.
In the tapestry of night,
Echoes keep our dreams in sight.

Stars above us boldly shine,
In their light, your hand in mine.
Together through the ebb and flow,
Echoes of forever, always know.

With every dawn, a brand new start,
Holding tightly to our hearts.
As shadows wane, our spirits soar,
In the echoes of forever, we explore.

In the Garden of Tender Moments

Petals whisper in the breeze,
Every touch, a heart's appease.
Underneath the blooming skies,
Love's pure essence gently lies.

In the garden, we find our space,
Tender moments, a warm embrace.
Gentle raindrops bless the ground,
In this haven, peace is found.

Colors dance in vibrant hues,
Nature's song, a sweet muse.
Hand in hand, we plant our dreams,
In the garden, life redeems.

Softly, sunbeams kiss our skin,
Each new day, where love begins.
Amidst the blooms, we stand tall,
In the garden, we cherish all.

Seasons change, but love stays bright,
In our hearts, it takes its flight.
Through every bud, our hopes arise,
In the garden beneath the skies.

Reaching for the Sun Together

Hands entwined, we chase the light,
Through the shadows, hearts take flight.
Every step, a dream in tow,
Reaching for the sun's warm glow.

Fields of gold stretch far and wide,
In this journey, side by side.
With each hurdle, we rise anew,
Reaching for the sun, me and you.

Mountains high, and valleys low,
Together, we will bravely go.
In the distance, hopes align,
Reaching for the sun, our hearts entwine.

Together facing fears that roam,
In each other, we've found home.
With every breath, our spirits sing,
Reaching for the sun, oh what joy it brings.

Through the night and into dawn,
With every sunrise, love goes on.
In the warmth of the bright day's hue,
Reaching for the sun, forever true.

Threads of Shared Dreams

Woven whispers of hope and care,
In the fabric of love we share.
Every thread holds a story dear,
Tales of joy, of laughter, and tears.

In the quiet, our dreams intertwine,
Connecting souls, your heart and mine.
Stitched in the moments, bright and bold,
Threads of dreams that never grow old.

Through the trials, we find our way,
Holding tight to the vows we say.
In this tapestry, we both belong,
Threads of shared dreams, forever strong.

Colors blend in the dance of fate,
Each brush of life, we craft and create.
With every stitch, we build anew,
Threads of shared dreams, me and you.

As the years weave their gentle lace,
In our hearts, a sacred space.
Together, we'll journey, hand in hand,
Threads of shared dreams across the land.

Beyond the Horizon of Together

We wander hand in hand, so free,
With dreams that stretch beyond the sea.
In twilight's glow, our shadows dance,
With every heartbeat, there's a chance.

Through whispered winds and rustling leaves,
Our hopes entwined, as the heart believes.
Each sunset paints a brand new sky,
Together, love will never die.

We chase the stars in velvet night,
In silent vows, our spirits' flight.
With every dawn, we find our way,
A journey bright, come what may.

Beyond the horizon, love's embrace,
A timeless song, a sacred place.
With laughter's echoes, soft and clear,
In every moment, you are near.

So let us dance, let the world fade,
In unity, our fears invades.
Beyond the horizon, dreams take wing,
In every beat, our hearts will sing.

The Nature of Our Connection

In gentle threads, our lives entwine,
A tapestry of love divine.
With every glance, a spark ignites,
In simple words, we share our sights.

A river flows where thoughts unite,
Through laughter's warmth, we share the light.
With whispers soft, and hands that hold,
We paint our stories, brave and bold.

Through seasons change, our bond renews,
Each moment's gift, a path we choose.
In silence shared, our spirits blend,
In every heartbeat, love transcends.

Your voice is like a melody,
That lingers sweetly, endlessly.
In every step, we find our grace,
In tender glances, love's embrace.

Together we'll explore the vast,
The nature of our hearts amassed.
With every day, we grow and learn,
In journeys shared, our spirits burn.

Unraveling the Mysteries of Us

In shadows cast, our secrets lie,
Wrapped in trust, like stars in sky.
Each question asked, a thread to pull,
While silence speaks, our hearts are full.

With every laugh, a truth unfolds,
Within our tales, the warmth it holds.
In dreams exchanged, we seek the same,
Unraveling joy, igniting flame.

As time unveils the layers thin,
In depths we wander, souls akin.
Through whispered nights and blazing days,
We find the path in myriad ways.

In every glance, a hint reveals,
The beautiful dance that love conceals.
We are the questions, we are the clues,
Unraveling mysteries, all we choose.

So hand in hand, we'll find the light,
In laughter shared, and love's delight.
Together we'll weave through the unknown,
In every heartbeat, we have grown.

Seasons of Shared Laughter

In spring's embrace, we bloom anew,
With laughter bright in skies so blue.
Each moment shared, a fleeting ray,
In joyful hearts, we dance and play.

Through summer's warmth, the sun so bright,
Our laughter echoes through the night.
With stories told 'neath starlit skies,
In every laugh, our spirit flies.

As autumn leaves begin to fall,
In laughter's sound, we heed the call.
With every whisper, breezes share,
In joyful bonds, we show we care.

In winter's chill, we find the fire,
With laughter near, our hearts conspire.
In cozy nooks, we knit our dreams,
With simple joys, or so it seems.

These seasons blend, a canvas bright,
With laughter's touch, we share the light.
Through every phase, our hearts will sing,
In shared laughter, love's offering.

When Time Stood Still

In the hush of moments past,
We lingered where shadows cast.
The world around began to fade,
As silence spoke, our hearts conveyed.

A clock with hands that dared to wait,
Every heartbeat sealed our fate.
Lost in the gaze we could not break,
A universe for us to make.

Each whisper floated on the breeze,
A timeless dance beneath the trees.
With every glance, the stars aligned,
In that stillness, love defined.

The world stood still, and so did we,
A memory etched in reverie.
In the pause of life, we learned to feel,
In moments lost, we made it real.

And though the hours march along,
We hold on tight to where we belong.
When time stood still, we found our way,
In the silence, forever stay.

Glances Across the Room

In crowded spaces, eyes collide,
A flicker here, a spark inside.
Silent stories in starlit night,
Unspoken words in shared delight.

Between the laughter, glances pass,
A moment caught, like fragile glass.
The heartbeat races, time suspends,
In fleeting looks, the mystery bends.

A world apart yet close in dreams,
In every gaze, the hope redeems.
With every smile, the pages turn,
As kindling ignites, we silently yearn.

Across the room, a whispered fate,
The distance fades, we contemplate.
In stolen seconds, time unwinds,
And in those eyes, our worlds align.

Each glance becomes a thread that weaves,
A tapestry of love, it cleaves.
Together, in this dance we find,
The magic sparked in hearts combined.

The Echo of Touch

Fingers brushed like whispers soft,
In the night where our spirits loft.
A spark ignites with every caress,
In that moment, we find our bliss.

The warmth of skin, a gentle fire,
Unraveling souls, lifting higher.
In the silence, pulses race,
The world dissolves, just us in space.

Every caress, a melody sweet,
In echoes soft we feel complete.
With tender strokes, we paint the air,
In this embrace, we share our care.

As shadows dance upon the wall,
In every touch, we heed the call.
A language of the heart, refined,
In this connection, bliss defined.

The echo of touch, forever last,
In memories held, a love steadfast.
Through every heartbeat, every sigh,
Together always, you and I.

Chains of Tenderness

In gentle binds that love creates,
We wrap our hearts in tender fates.
Each moment held in soft embrace,
The chains we forge, our sacred space.

With every laughter, every tear,
These links grow strong, we persevere.
A bond of warmth that never breaks,
Through trials faced and paths we take.

In every whisper, promises made,
A tapestry of love displayed.
Though storms may come and shadows loom,
In chains of tenderness, we bloom.

Together forged, our hearts in sync,
The trust we build, a sacred link.
With every breath, we intertwine,
In this connection, hearts divine.

These chains we wear, not made of strife,
But tender ties that shape our life.
In every moment shared and sweet,
Chains of tenderness make us complete.

Fleeting Glances

In crowded rooms, our eyes meet,
A spark ignites, a silent heat.
Moments shared, then lost in time,
A fleeting glance, a whispered rhyme.

Through passing streets, your shadow sways,
A fleeting touch that softly stays.
In busy lives, we drift apart,
Yet echoes linger in my heart.

Under moonlit skies, we roam,
Each glance a thread, we call it home.
In the chaos, a pause we find,
Fleeting glimpses, forever enshrined.

And though the years may take their toll,
Those glances carved within my soul.
In memories brief, love holds its grace,
A timeless dance in a crowded space.

So here we stand, beneath the stars,
Collecting glances like hidden scars.
In every gaze, a world is spun,
Fleeting moments, but never done.

Lasting Memories

In quiet corners, time stands still,
We weave our stories, heart and will.
A photograph, a whispered laugh,
Lasting memories on our path.

Through seasons changing, we have grown,
In shared laughter, love has shown.
Each moment cherished, brush with fate,
In our hearts, they resonate.

The scent of rain, the morning light,
Every detail feels so right.
A touch, a word, a simple sign,
In lasting memories, love aligns.

From whispered tales to starlit dreams,
Each lasting memory softly gleams.
Time may fade, but we will cling,
To sweet reminders that life can bring.

In twilight hours, we sit and share,
The stories woven with utmost care.
In every heart, where love still grows,
Lasting memories weave like prose.

The Essence of Us

In gentle whispers, dreams take flight,
The essence of us, a pure delight.
With every heartbeat, we align,
A dance of souls, forever intertwined.

In secret glances, promises fold,
The essence of us, a story told.
Through sun-kissed days and starry nights,
Our love unfolds, like soaring kites.

In tender moments, laughter rings,
The essence of us, in simple things.
With every touch, a spark ignites,
Creating warmth on chilly nights.

Through storms that come, and shadows cast,
The essence of us remains steadfast.
In trials faced and hurdles tall,
Our love endures, it conquers all.

As seasons change, we find our way,
The essence of us will always stay.
In every heartbeat, every sigh,
We weave our love, a lullaby.

Threads of Light in Shadowed Days

In darkest hours, a flicker gleams,
Threads of light ignite our dreams.
Through shadowed paths, we walk with grace,
Finding joy in a sacred space.

Each tiny spark, a beacon bright,
Threads of light dispelling night.
In silver linings, hope reveals,
A promise made, a heart that heals.

With every tear, a lesson learned,
Threads of light in darkness burned.
In laughter shared, our spirits soar,
A tapestry of love we pour.

Through trials faced, we rise anew,
Threads of light will guide us through.
In every challenge, we find a way,
Boldly shining on shadowed days.

So let us cherish every ray,
Threads of light will never stray.
In moments small, joy finds its place,
Even in shadows, love embraces.

An Invitation to Eternity

In whispered vows beneath the stars,
An invitation to love that's ours.
With every promise, hearts entwined,
A journey infinite, beautifully blind.

Through time and space, we'll dance and weave,
An invitation to never leave.
In every glance, a world expands,
Together we rise, hand in hand.

With every heartbeat, love renews,
An invitation to choose the hues.
Painting our lives with vibrant dreams,
Eternity flows in endless streams.

As seasons shift and years unfold,
An invitation to stories told.
With each sunrise, a chance to grow,
In love's embrace, we'll forever glow.

In every moment, let's celebrate,
An invitation to love, innate.
With every breath, a sweet decree,
Eternity beckons, you and me.

The Architecture of Our Bond

In shadows cast, we build our dreams,
With bricks of trust, or so it seems.
Each laughter shared, each whispered thought,
Lays down the path that love has wrought.

Through storm and sun, our pillars stand,
Together strong, we face the land.
With every stone, a memory made,
An edifice that will not fade.

The arches curve, our hearts align,
In every glance, a silent sign.
Blueprints drawn in whispered night,
A sacred space, both warm and bright.

Foundations set in hope and grace,
In ancient tales, we find our place.
With every breath, we carve our way,
In love's sweet grip, forever stay.

Thus built our bond, a sturdy frame,
With endless love, our hearts proclaim.
A dwelling strong, through thick and thin,
In this grand space, the joy begins.

The Language Only We Speak

In glances shared, we find our sound,
A melody where hearts are bound.
In every pause, a story told,
In silent vows, our truths unfold.

The rustle of leaves, the softest sigh,
A symphony under the open sky.
In whispered dreams, our voices blend,
A language bright, no need to pretend.

In every heartbeat, we find the verse,
A rhythm sweet, we both rehearse.
The notes we play are pure and real,
In every silence, we silently feel.

With secret laughs and knowing looks,
We weave the lines from unwritten books.
In every heartbeat, the world takes pause,
In our embrace, life finds its cause.

Thus in this dance, we find our way,
A language crafted for every day.
In laughter's echo, joy takes flight,
Together we shine, a shared light.

Celestial Threads of Affinity

Under stars, our spirits twine,
In cosmic dance, our hearts align.
With every wish upon the night,
We find our place, in love's pure light.

The moonlit paths where dreams converge,
In gentle tides, our souls emerge.
Each heartbeat feels like stardust whirls,
In this vast space, our magic twirls.

With every dawn, a new thread spun,
In golden rays, two lives are one.
The universe hums a song so sweet,
A final note where we both meet.

In nebulae, our hopes ignite,
A tapestry of dark and light.
Each star a promise, glowing bright,
In endless skies, we take our flight.

Bound by the cosmos, ever strong,
Together we write our endless song.
In love's embrace, we journey far,
Two souls entwined, like a guiding star.

Our Journey Beyond Time

In footsteps laid on sands of gold,
Together we walk, our story unfolds.
With every mile, the moments grow,
In whispered winds, love's river flows.

From dawn till dusk, our hearts explore,
Across the years, we seek for more.
In laughter bright and shadows cast,
We find the strength that holds us fast.

Through valleys deep and mountains high,
With every breath, we touch the sky.
Each twist and turn, an adventure new,
In this vast world, it's me and you.

Time holds no bounds, it bends and sways,
In timeless moments, love always stays.
With every glance, eternity calls,
In the fabric of life, our bond enthralls.

As seasons change, our spirits rise,
In every sunset, love never dies.
Together we roam, hand in hand,
In this journey grand, we understand.

Hearts in Bloom

In gardens where the wildflowers sway,
Hearts awaken with the break of day.
Petals dance in the soft spring air,
Every moment, a promise laid bare.

Sunlight kisses the morning dew,
Whispers of love blossom anew.
Breezes carry sweet songs of cheer,
While hopes and dreams draw ever near.

Colors blend in a vibrant display,
Nature's way to celebrate the play.
Each bloom tells a story untold,
In vibrant hues of red and gold.

Time lingers where laughter resides,
Among the blooms where love abides.
In the warmth of the sun's gentle gaze,
Two hearts intertwined in endless maze.

When twilight arrives with a sigh,
Stars emerge from the canvas sky.
Hearts in bloom, forever entwined,
In nature's embrace, their souls aligned.

Whispers of Togetherness

In the quiet moments we find our peace,
Whispers of love that never cease.
Hand in hand, we'll wander far,
Together beneath the same bright star.

In laughter shared and gentle sighs,
Time becomes the friend that flies.
Every glance, a secret spoken,
In the tapestry of trust unbroken.

Softly, the night wraps us tight,
Creating shadows with soft, warm light.
In every heartbeat, we feel the tune,
A melody sweet as the silvery moon.

Every challenge, together we face,
In our haven, we find our place.
With you, each day feels so right,
Whispers of love, our guiding light.

Through storms we stand, unyielding, true,
In the shelter of me, I'll find you.
In every silence, our spirits soar,
Whispers of togetherness forevermore.

Echoes of Desire

In the night where secrets weave,
Echoes whisper what we believe.
Burning flames in shadows cast,
Every glance, a spell is cast.

In stolen moments, hearts collide,
Through the darkness, love will guide.
Silhouettes dance in the silver light,
United souls in the depths of night.

Every heartbeat resonates strong,
In passion's rhythm, we belong.
The air is thick with the scent of dreams,
In the silence, the universe teems.

Words unspoken fill the space,
In the warmth of your sweet embrace.
Echoes of desire in every sigh,
Boundless wishes that will not die.

In twilight's hold, temptation grows,
In wild affection, our spirit flows.
Together we'll chase the stars above,
In the echoes of our endless love.

Tapestry of Us

In the fabric of life, we find our thread,
Woven together where hearts have tread.
Every color a memory shared,
In this tapestry, we've truly dared.

With each stitch, our story unfolds,
In laughter and tears, our journey told.
Threads of hope sewn next to fear,
Creating a pattern, unique and clear.

Intertwined, through thick and thin,
In the dance of life, we twirl and spin.
Every moment a delicate hue,
In the tapestry, it's me and you.

Through storms and calm, we hold on tight,
Embroidered dreams shine in the night.
Together we are both bold and bright,
A masterpiece crafted in pure delight.

As the years pass, the colors evolve,
In the warmth of love, our spirits resolve.
Woven eternally, we softly sing,
In the tapestry of us, endless spring.

The Sanctuary of Your Embrace

In the hush of twilight's glow,
Your arms wrap tight, a tender place.
Every heartbeat, a gentle flow,
In this sanctuary, I find grace.

Time slows down, the world, a blur,
Murmuting fears, we breathe as one.
With every whisper, love's soft stir,
Under the stars, we're never done.

Your laughter dances on the air,
A melody that warms my soul.
In your presence, I feel so rare,
A perfect bliss that makes me whole.

Moments shared, like petals fall,
Each a memory, brighter than gold.
In the echo of our call,
Our story blooms, forever told.

So let the night wrap us in light,
In this embrace, we find our home.
Together, we take flight,
Wherever love may lead, we roam.

A Canvas Painted with Moments

Brushstrokes of laughter, colors bright,
Each memory, a vivid hue.
Life's canvas, a beautiful sight,
Every moment, a masterpiece true.

Whispers of the past intertwine,
In the corners of my mind's view.
Time stands still, like sweet red wine,
Memories linger, sparkling and new.

We dance through days, hand in hand,
Creating portraits of joy and grace.
In this gallery, we boldly stand,
Each smile a frame, each tear a trace.

Sunsets blend in soft embrace,
With each brush, a story we'll tell.
In this world, we've found our place,
A canvas where love casts its spell.

So let your heart paint what it sees,
In vibrant tones and softest light.
Each moment crafted, hearts at ease,
In this gallery, everything feels right.

Serenade of Sweet Whispers

In the silence, whispers play,
Secrets shared in tender tone.
Every word, a soft ballet,
In the night, we feel alone.

Stars above our quiet song,
Echoes of a gentle breeze.
With you, I know I belong,
In this moment, hearts at ease.

Your breath is music to my soul,
Each sigh a note of pure delight.
Together, we can be whole,
Wrapped in shadows, kissed by light.

The world outside may fade away,
Here, secrets dance beneath the moon.
Forever in this sweet array,
I cherish every whispered tune.

So let us linger, let time freeze,
In this serenade, love's embrace.
With every whisper, gentle breeze,
We create a timeless space.

Beneath the Canopy of Trust

Underneath the branches wide,
We find solace, dreams take flight.
In this haven, hearts confide,
Holding secrets in the night.

Leaves rustle with tales we weave,
Every story, a thread of gold.
In our bond, we truly believe,
Trust is a treasure, brave and bold.

The sun peeks through, warm and bright,
Casting shadows of hope and cheer.
Together, we embrace the light,
With every glance, I hold you near.

This refuge, a sacred place,
Where vulnerabilities thrive.
In each moment, we interlace,
Building roots, love will survive.

So let us dwell, forever here,
Beneath the canopy, hearts aligned.
In this space, we conquer fear,
In trust's embrace, our souls entwined.

Radiance in Your Smile

Your smile lights up the day,
Chasing the shadows away.
In every glance, warmth flows,
A gentle light that ever glows.

The sun pales in your grace,
A shining star in this space.
In laughter, we find our bliss,
Moments captured with a kiss.

Each joy shared feels so bright,
A beacon in the night.
Through storms, your smile remains,
A promise that forever sustains.

With every fleeting glance,
You invite my heart to dance.
Your radiance, pure and true,
A masterpiece, just me and you.

In your eyes, I see a flame,
Igniting love, never the same.
A sparkle that draws me near,
With you, my path is always clear.

Cherished Moments

In the stillness, time stands still,
Each second, a treasure to fill.
We gather memories in our hearts,
Crafting stories, a work of art.

Laughter echoes in the air,
Each moment, beyond compare.
Whispers shared beneath the stars,
Bonding us, no matter how far.

Through quiet nights and sunny days,
Our laughter dances in joyful ways.
Time flows like a gentle stream,
Every moment, a cherished dream.

The little things, a loving touch,
I cherish them all so much.
Your voice, a melody I know,
In every whisper, love does grow.

Life's canvas painted bright and clear,
With every moment spent so dear.
Hand in hand, we'll face the night,
Now and always, hearts alight.

Infinite Together

In a world where time is fleeting,
Our love stands strong, unyielding,
Two souls merging, boundless flight,
Infinite together, pure delight.

Each heartbeat sings a song,
In harmony, we both belong.
Moments woven, side by side,
In this journey, love our guide.

Mountains may rise, rivers flow,
Through it all, our bond will grow.
With every twilight, morning's light,
We find joy in simple sight.

Together we craft our destiny,
A tapestry, you and me.
In laughter, tears, we'll always share,
An infinite love beyond compare.

In every dusk, a promise made,
In brighter days, our dreams cascade.
Together, we paint the skies,
With each moment, love never dies.

The Canvas of Us

With colors bold and hues so bright,
We paint our dreams, day and night.
Each brushstroke tells a tale anew,
On the canvas, just me and you.

Every laugh a splash of gold,
In our gallery, stories unfold.
Moments captured, a vivid array,
In the art of love, we find our way.

A swirl of hopes, a blend of fears,
Together, we've crafted the years.
With every color, a piece of our soul,
In this masterpiece, we are whole.

The canvas awaits, untouched, pristine,
For every dream we dare to glean.
With every stroke, our spirits soar,
Creating memories forevermore.

Together, we'll paint our forever,
In a gallery, fading never.
The canvas of us, strong and bright,
Our love, a work of pure delight.